Dal buio alla luce

original story:
Jennifer Degenhardt

translator:
Dr. Tanya Ferretto

illustrator:
Juliette Chattaway

This story is for all who experience challenges with their mental health.
May you find your ray of sunshine.

AUTHOR'S NOTE

Hello!

Thank you for taking the time to read this message before you start reading. It's important that you know what you might find in the pages so you can make a reasonable choice whether or not to dive in.

This story deals with inner turmoil and associated dark thoughts, up to and including those of self-harm. I did not write this story to be triggering to anyone, but rather - as always - to provide an opportunity for discussion. It is my hope that by sharing a story that is based on feelings that I have had personally, that I can help with the discussion about self-harm, suicidal thoughts and the spiral that the human mind can get itself into. Yes, you read that right: I have struggled with depression and delicate mental health for many years, which ultimately led to some really negative thinking. While it is not a time in my life that I wish to revisit, I am grateful for the experience, as it has changed the way I view everything in life.

The first and best thing I did was to ask for help. And I didn't just ask one person, I asked many. Family and friends were there for me, as I know that family and friends would be for anyone - if the person in need simply asks for help.

This story is meant to serve as a jumping-off point to talk about mental health and to provide one look into the anxiety that some experience. Furthermore, since each person's journey is different, the novel ends with possibility. In no way does the ending mean to suggest that struggles such as these can be easily taken care of with an ice cream, a flower or even a puppy. Still, I wanted to end with some hope for better days - like the ones I am so fortunate enough to experience now.

The subject matter is difficult. Please read with care.

-Jen Degenhardt
July 2023

You aren't going to feel this way forever, you know.

The mind has thoughts, and those thoughts control your feelings.

It will all be okay in the end. If it's not okay, it's not the end.

Try to think positively. Everything in life - including the bad - is temporary.

I imagine that your path in life will be a little difficult for a while, but it won't be forever. Everything will get better.

Remember: your thoughts control your feelings. And you can change your thoughts.

RINGRAZIAMENTI

Having had this story in mind for a while, I started it on the plane on a return flight from California, I think it was. I had done the preparation, taken the notes and had begun writing furiously. And then somehow, I deleted the file. Like, really deleted it, not just in file purgatory. Ugh.

But I had already hired the artist. Juliet Chattaway was still in elementary school when I asked her to draw a teenager in a hoodie, in a bedroom with one window. I then asked her to alter the drawings a bit at a time (I don't want to give it away!), so they too, could be part of the story. Juliet understood my vision exactly, even when I might not always have been so clear. It is a pleasure and an honor to work with student artists like Juliet. They are offered a unique opportunity, and I get to help them realize that "business" doesn't have to be scary. It's a win-win. Many, many thanks to Juliet for her awesome artwork, but also for her patience. Due to - well, life - this novel took longer than I anticipated to get published. Thank you, Juliet!

You are reading this version in Italian thanks to Tanya Ferretto, Ph.D., a native Italian speaker and high school Italian teacher. It is a joy to work with Tanya, not only for her expertise, but for her genuine care about the themes of my books and her overall empathy for humans and other beings.

Thank you, Tanya, for helping this message get to even more readers.

I owe the following people a huge debt of gratitude (and if you're reading this, or any of my books, so do you. 😌) If not for these people to whom I reached out for help those few years ago, I may not have had the opportunity to write this story - or any others for that matter. I am grateful to each of you. Thank you.

Sarah Jessup & Robert Allen

Celia Bartholomew & John Bartholomew

Angela Degenhardt

Claire Degrigrio

Tara Allen & José Salazar

Amy Salvin Collins

Wendy Perrotti

Patti Nietsch

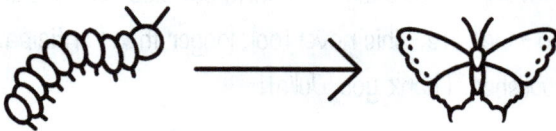

Just when the caterpillar thought the world was over, it became a butterfly...

-proverb

In una casa ...

o appartamento ...

o un condominio ...

La zia bussa alla porta.

Ale, posso entrare?

La zia apre un po' la porta. Ale è sul pavimento, in una stanza buia, vicino al letto.

La zia apre la porta un po'
di più.

Sì, Zia. Sto bene.
Più o meno.

Lascia che tiri su la persiana per far entrare il sole.

No, Zia preferisco restare al buio.

OK, Ale. Devo uscire per un'ora. Vuoi venire con me? Possiamo comprare le tue caramelle preferite, come facevamo una volta...

OK. Veramente stai bene? Non voglio lasciarti...

Andrà via. Passerà.
Vedrai. Ci vediamo
tra un'oretta.
Riposati.

A dopo, Zia.

La verità è che non voglio sentirmi in questo modo. Questi sentimenti mi stanno facendo soffrire. Ma quello che è successo non era colpa mia...

Ma io non avevo chiesto di ricevere lezioni così costose. Avrei preferito allenarmi ad un livello più basso...

Sì, LO SO. LO SO! È vero che lo sapevo. E sì, volevo continuare. Volevo tutto.

Non ho preso io i soldi dal suo cliente. Mio padre lo ha fatto. E ha detto che voleva restituirli.

Non è un criminale. Ha fatto una cosa brutta, ma non è un criminale.

42

Non parlarmi in quel modo. Sono un adolescente. Non sono un adulto. Non faccio tutto sbagliato. Sii gentile con me. Non è colpa mia.

44

No, no! NO! Questo è doloroso, e non riesco a pensare chiaramente. Vai via! Non voglio più parlare con te. Sono giovan...

Ale comincia a piangere.

49

50

Voglio che la mia vita sia com'era prima. Voglio avere i miei genitori con me e voglio avere solo problemi come un compito di scienza o un'altra competizione.

Ti sei allenato così tanto che ti sei fatto male. Così i tuoi genitori hanno dovuto pagare ancora più soldi: al centro degli allenamenti e all'ospedale. E tu sapevi che non avevano abbastanza soldi...

58

60

È vero.
È vero che sei triste. Prima vivevi una
una vita senza problemi, ma adesso non è
più così. Adesso non sei più con i tuoi
genitori perché i loro problemi sono colpa
tua.

64

66

69

72

78

79

81

Ale piange.

Ale prende la bottiglietta con le pastiglie dentro. L'unica cosa che si sente sono i singhiozzi – i singhiozzi di una persona che prova un dolore così grande. Una persona che non ha più forza...

Ale tiene in mano la bottiglia con le pastiglie quando crolla.

Pasa molto tempo.

La zia arriva a casa. Porta con sé una scatola.

Non sente alcuna risposta.
L'unica cosa che si sente
sono i rumori del cucciolo.

bau ! bau !

La zia va nella camera di Ale. Ale è per terra con la bottiglia di pastiglie accanto.

La zia mette giù la scatola con il cucciolo e corre dove si trova Ale.

Gli occhi di Ale si aprono un po'.

No, Zia. Non le ho prese.

Oh, Ale. Non ti preoccupare. Tutto si sistemerà. I problemi si risolveranno.

100

Ale, non è colpa tua. Queste cose succcedono nella vita. Tuo papà è un adulto, e ha preso le sue decisioni.

Ma ha rubato dal cliente per pagare per i miei allenamenti. E a causa di quel crimine mia mamma ha cominciato a bere sempre di più...

Speriamo che terranno in considerazione quanto è successo e prenderanno decisioni migliori.

Proprio in quel momento, il cucciolo comincia ad abbaiare di nuovo.

Quando ero giovane, avevo un cane che si chiamava Sole.

La zia porta la scatola e la apre. Il cucciolo salta fuori e va subito da Ale.

Atena. La chiamerò Atena. Atena era la divinità della forza e del coraggio. Quel nome mi aiuterà molto.

Ricordati questo modo di dire: "Alla fine andrà tutto bene. Se non va bene, allora non è la fine."

Da un'amica, un'amica molto saggia ed intelligente.

E guarda, c'è il sole fuori. Cose ne dici di andare fuori con Atena così può conoscere il suo nuovo vicinato?

Hey there!
If you need help, or a friend needs help, tell someone. Find a trusted adult who can help, too. And, check out the resources below.
☮❤😊

Suicide and Crisis Lifeline
988 – via phone or text

The Crisis Text Line
Text TALK to 741741

The American Foundation for Suicide Prevention
https://afsp.org/get-help

Outside of the USA
Find a Helpline
https://findahelpline.com/i/iasp
127

GLOSSARIO

A

a - at, to
abbaiare - to bark
abbastanza - quite a bit
abisso - abyss
accanto - near
ad - at, to
adesso - now
adolescente - teen
adorabile - adorable
adulti - adults
adulto - adult
affrontare - to face
ai - to the
aiuta - s/he, it helps
aiutarmi - to help me
aiutarti - to help you
aiutato - helped
aiuterà - s/he, it will help
aiuteranno - they will help
aiuterebbe - s/he, it would help
aiuti - you help
aiuto - I help
alcun/a - some
al/all'/allo/ai/agli/all a/alle- to the

allenamenti - sport practice
allenarmi - I do sport practice
allenarti - you do sport practice
allenato - trained
allenatore - trainer
allora - so
altra - other
altri - others
amica/o - friend
ammettere - to admit
anche - also
ancora - more
andare - to go
andiamo - we go
andrà - s/he, it will go
ansia - anxiety
appartamento - apartment
apre - s/he, it opens
aprono - they open
arrestato - arrested
arresto - arrest
arriva - s/he, it arrives
Atena - name of a deity
attaccano - attack; attach
attuale - now
auto - self

auto-medicarsi - self-medicate

avanti - ahead

avere - to have

avessi - that I have

aveva - s/he, it had

avevano - they had

avevo - I had

avrebbe - s/he, it would have

avrei - I would have

B

basso - low

bel - nice

bene - well

bere - to drink

beveva - s/he, it drank

(hai) bisogno - you need

bloccare - to block

borsa - bag

bottiglia - bottle

bottiglietta - small bottle

bravo - good at, skilled

brutta/o/i/e - ugly

bugie - lies

buia/o - dark

buono - good

bussa - s/he, it knocks

C

camera - room

cane - dog

caramelle - candies

carina - nice

casa - house

(a) causa - because of

causato - caused

(non) ce (la faccio) - I can't do it, I can't take it

centro - center

cerca - s/he, it looks for

certe - certain

certo - sure

cervello - brain

che - that

chi - who

chiamato - called

chiamava - called

chiamerà - s/he, it will call

chiamerai - you will call

chiaramente - clearly

chiedendo - asking

chiedo - I ask

chiesto - asked

ci (vediamo) - we see each other

cliente - client
codardo - coward
colpa - fault
com'(era) - how it
 was
come - how
comincia - s/he, it
 starts
cominciato - started
competizione -
 competition
compito - test
complicata -
 complicated
comprare - to buy
comprensione -
 understanding
con - with
condominio -
 condominium
conoscere - to know
considerazione -
 consideration
continuare - to
 continue
controllano - they
 control
controllo - the
 check, control
coooooosa - whaaaat
coraggio - courage
corpo - body
corre - s/he, it runs
cosa - what, thing
cose - things

così - in that way
costavano - cost
costo - cost
costosa/o/i/e -
 costly
criminale -
 criminal
crimine - crime
crolla - falls down
cucciolo - puppy
cui - which

D

da - from
dal - from the
darmi - to give me
davvero - really
decisioni -
 decisions
degli - of the
dei - of the
del - of the
della - of the
dentro - inside
depressione -
 depression
depresso - depressed
(ha) detto - s/he, it
 said
devi - you have to,
 must
devo - I have to,
 must
di - of

(che tu mi) dia - that you give me

dice - s/he, it says

dici - you say

difficile - difficult

dillo - say it

dimenticarmi - to forget

dimenticarsi - to forget

dimenticarti - you forget

dimmi - tell me

dire - to say

distruzione - destruction

disturbarmi - to bother me

disturbino - to bother me

diventare - to become

divinità - divinity

do - I give

dolore - pain

doloroso - painful

dopo - after

dove - where

dovevano - they had to

dovrai - you will have to

dovresti - you should

(hanno) dovuto - they had

dubito - I doubt

E

e - and

è - is

ecco - here is

economici - cheap

ed - and

enorme - huge

entrare - to enter

entrata - entrance

era - s/he, it was

erano - they were

eri - you were

ero - I was

esattamente - exactly

esempio - example

essere - to be

(dopo) essermi (fatto male) - after having hurt myself

F

facciamo - we make

faccio - I make

(non ce la) faccio (più) - I can't take it anymore

facendo - making

(non ce la) faceva - s/he, it couldn't make it

132

**(come) facevamo
(una volta) -** like we
used to do
facevi - you did
famiglia - family
fammelo (vedere) -
let me see
fanno (soffrire) -
they make me
suffer
far (entrare la luce) -
to let the light in
farai - you will do it
fare - to do, to make
farlo - to do it
farmi (del male) - to
hurt myself
farti (del male) -
hurt yourself
fatto - done
felice - happy
femmina - female
(si) fida - s/he, it
trusts
finché - until when
fine - end
fino - up to
forse - maybe
forza - strength
fossi - that you were
fratello - brother
fuori - out
futuro - future

G
genitori - parents
gentile - kind
giovane - young
giusto - correct
gli - the
(saresti in) grado -
you would be able
to
grande - big
grazie - thank you
guarda - look
guardati - look at
yourself
guardavano - they
looked

H
ha - s/he,it has
hai - you have
hanno - they have
ho - I have

I
i - the
idea - idea
il - the
immaginare - to
imagine
in - in
inoltre - moreover
intelligente -
intelligent

133

intendi - you mean
interiore - interior
inutile - useless
io - I

L
l' - the
la - the
lascerò - I will leave
lascia - s/he it
lasciarmi - to leave me
lasciarti - to leave you
le - the
lei - she
letto - bed
lezioni - lessons
liberarti - to free yourself
livello - level
lo - the
loro - they
lui - he

M
ma - but
madre - mother
male - badly
malissimo - very badly
mamma - mom

mandami - send me
mano - hand
maschio - male
me - me
medicarsi - medicate oneself
medicina - medicine
medicine - medicines
meglio - better
meno - less
mentale - mental
mente - mind
mentendo - lying
mentre - while
messaggino - text message
mette - s/he it puts
mi - to me
mia - my
miei - my
migliorare - to improve
migliore - better
migliorerà - it will improve
migliori - better
mio - my; mine
modo - way
molto - a lot
momento - moment
motivo - reason

N

ne - of it
neghi - you deny
nel - in the
nella - in the
nemmeno - not even
niente - nothing
no - no
nome - name
non - not
nulla - nothing
nuovo - new

O

o - or
occhi - eyes
ogni - each
OK - okay
ora - hour
oretta - short hour
ospedale - hospital
ottenere - obtain
ottima - excellent
ovvio - obvious

P

padre - father
pagare - to pay
papà - dad
paratecipare - to participate
parlami - to talk to me
parlare - to talk

parlarmi - to talk to me
partecipare - to participate
partecipato - participated
particolarmente - particularly
passa – s/he, it passes
passavo - I passed
passerà - it will pass
pastiglia - pill
pavimento - floor
peccato - shame
pensaci - think about it
pensare - to think
pensato - thought
pensi - you think
pensieri - thoughts
penso - I think
per - for; in order to
perché - because; why
percorso - journey
perfetta - perfect
perfezione - perfection
periodo - period
persiana - shutter
persona - person
peso - weight
più - more
piacciono - like

piace - like
piaceva - liked
pianga - that you cry
piangendo - crying
piangere - to cry
piangi - you cry
piani - plans
piano - plan
piccolino - little one
più - more
po' - a little; little
pochino - small amount
poi - then
polizia - police
porta - s/he,it brings
positivo - positive
possiamo - we can
posso - I can
potesse - that s/he it could
poteva - s/he, it was able to
potuto - could
povero - poor
preferisco - I prefer
preferite - you (plural) prefer
(avrei) preferito - I would have preferred
(ti) prego - I beg you
prende - s/he, it takes

prenderanno - they will take
prendere - to take
prenderla - to take it
(se tu) prendessi - if you took
prendi - you take
preoccupare - to worry
prese - taken
presentato - presented
preso - taken
prigione - prison
prima - before
problemi - problems
pronta - ready
a proposito - speaking of
proprio - just
prova - feels
può - s/he,it can
punto - point
puoi - you can

Q
qualcosa - something
quando - when
quanto - how much
quei - those
quel - that
quelle - those
quello - that
questo/a/e/i - this/these

qui - here
quindi - therefore, so

R

razionalmente -
　rationally
reale - real
(in) realtà -
　truthfully
restare - to stay
restituirli - to return
　them
resto - the rest
ricevere - to receive
ricordati - remember
ricordi - memories
riesci - to succeed
riesco - I succeed
riposati - you rest
risolveranno - they
　will resolve
risposta - answer
rubato - stolen
rumori - noises

S

saggia - wise
sai - you know
salta - s/he, it jumps
saperlo - to know it
sapevi - you knew
sapevo - I knew
sarà - it will be
sarai - you will be

sarebbe - s/he, it
　would be
saresti - you would
　be
sbagliato - wrong
scappare - to
　escape, run away
scatola - box
scienza - science
se - if
sé - one self
sei - you are
sempre - always
(si) sente - one hears
sentimenti - feelings
sentirò - I will feel
(ti) sentirai - you will
　feel
sentirmi - to feel
(mi) sento - I feel
senza - without
serve - is needed
sessioni - sessions
si - oneself; one
sia - is
sicura - safe
siete - you are
sii - be
silenzio - quiet
singhiozzi - sobs
(si) sistemerà - it
　will be ok
situazione/i -
　situation/s
smettere - to stop

smetti - stop
so - I know
sociali - social
soffrire - to suffer
soldi - money
sole - sun
solo - only
sono - I am; they are
sorpresa - surprise
spedito - sent
speriamo - we hope
sport - sport
stai - you are
stai (bene) - you are well
stanno (facendo soffrire) - are making you suffer
stanza - room
starò - I will be okay well
stare - to be; to stay
stata - it was
stato - it was
stavo - I was
sto - I am
studiato - studied
studio - I study
su - on
subito - right away
succcedono - they happen
succederà - it will happen
successe - happened

successivo - next
sue – his/ hers, their (3rd person singular)
sul - on the
suo - his/hers/their
suoi - his/hers/their
svegliati - wake up

T
tantissimo - so much
tanto - a lot
te - you
tempo - time
temporanee - temporary
(per) terra - on the floor
terranno – they will keep
ti - to you, you
tiene - s/he, it keeps
tiri (su) - you pull up
tornata - returned
(avere) torto - to be wrong
tra - in (with time)
triste - sad
troppo - too much
trova - s/he, it finds
tu - you
tua/o/oi/e - your
tutta/e/i/o - all

U

ubriacarsi - to get drunk
ultima - last
un - a
una - a
unica - only
università - university
uscirà - s/he, it will leave
uscire - to leave, exit

V

va - s/he, it goes
vai - you go
valore - value
vattene - go away
vedere - to see
vedi - you see
vediamo - we see
vedrai - you will see
venire - to come
veramente - truly
verità - truth
(è) vero - it is true
verso - toward
(va) via - go away
viaggio - trip
vicinato - neighborhood
vicino - near
vincendo - winning
vincere - to win

visto (che) - since
vita - life
vivere - to live
vivevi - you lived
voce - voice
voglio - I want
voleva - s/he, it wanted
volevi - you wanted
volevo - I wanted
volta/e - time (that you count)
vuoi - you want

Z

zia - aunt

ABOUT THE AUTHOR

Jennifer Degenhardt taught high school Spanish for over 20 years and now teaches at the college level. At the time she realized her own high school students, many of whom had learning challenges, acquired language best through stories, so she began to write ones that she thought would appeal to them. She has been writing ever since.

Other titles by Jen Degenhardt:

La chica nueva | *La Nouvelle Fille* | The New Girl | *Das Neue Mädchen* | *La nuova ragazza*

141

Con (un poco de) ayuda de mis amigos / With (a little) Help from My Friends | *Un petit coup de main amical*
Con (un po') d'aiuto dai miei amici
La última prueba | The Last Test
Los tres amigos | Three Friends | *Drei Freunde* | *Les trois amis*
La evolución musical
María María: un cuento de un huracán | María María: A Story of a Storm | *Maria Maria: un histoire d'un orage*
Debido a la tormenta / Because of the Storm
La lucha de la vida / The Fight of His Life
Secretos / Secrets
Como vuela la pelota
Cambios / *Changements* / Changes
De la oscuridad a la luz | From Darkness into Light | *Dal buio alla luce*
El pueblo | The Town

@JenniferDegenh|

@jendegenhardt9

@PuentesLanguage &
World Language Teaching Stories (group)

143

Visit www.puenteslanguage.com to sign up to receive information on new releases and other events.

Check out all titles as eBooks with audio on www.digilangua.co.

ABOUT THE ILLUSTRATOR

Juliet Chattaway is a sixth-grade student at New Canaan Country School. She has loved art all her life and draws after school every day. In addition to drawing, Juliet spends her free time reading and writing short stories. One day, she hopes to publish her own Webtoon or book. Juliet lives in Darien, CT with her mother, father and younger brother, Nicholas.

ABOUT THE TRANSLATOR

Dr. Tanya Ferretto. was born and educated in Venice, Italy, where she enjoyed reading, writing and the arts. She has a Ph.D. in Japanese Art history. For the past 15 years she has been an Italian teacher at Winchester High School, MA. Teaching is her passion.